Plymouth
in old picture postcards

by
Mary M. Davenport

European Library - Zaltbommel/Netherlands MCMLXXXV

GB   ISBN 90 288 2984 9 / CIP

European Library in Zaltbommel/Netherlands publishes among other things the following series:

IN OLD PICTURE POSTCARDS *is a series of books which sets out to show what a particular place looked like and what life was like in Victorian and Edwardian times. A book about virtually every town in the United Kingdom is to be published in this series. By the end of this year about 175 different volumes will have appeared. 1,250 books have already been published devoted to the Netherlands with the title* **In oude ansichten.** *In Germany, Austria and Switzerland 500, 60 and 15 books have been published as* **In alten Ansichten;** *in France by the name* **En cartes postales anciennes** *and in Belgium as* **En cartes postales anciennes** *and/or* **In oude prentkaarten** *150 respectively 400 volumes have been published.*

For further particulars about published or forthcoming books, apply to your bookseller or direct to the publisher.

This edition has been printed and bound by Grafisch Bedrijf De Steigerpoort in Zaltbommel/Netherlands.

INTRODUCTION

*A city of the sea and ships, with
a shoreline of infinite variety.*

Plymouth is a vibrant and exciting city, with a great historic past. You will find various pieces of local history scattered throughout the following pages, of people, places and events. Many legends and ancient myths abound from the early days of the settlement at Sutton Pool to the time the town took its name from the river Plym. It was in the fourteenth century that the friars moved into the area, giving their name to Black Friars Lane, and Black Friars House in Southside Street. In the sixteenth century Sir Walter Raleigh came here and sent ships at his own expense to colonise Virginia; from 1584 to 1586 the ships and pilgrims sailed from Plymouth for Roanoke Island, but these costly expeditions were not completely successful, and later expeditions could find no trace of the settlers. What happened is a great mystery. In the seventeenth century came the Huguenot refugees, craftsmen in many arts and crafts.

In 1620 the Pilgrim Fathers sailed, 150 brave souls who made history when they settled in the New World.

There is a time in Plymouth's history which is remembered throughout the world, this was during the reign of Queen Elizabeth I. In this era merchants built fine houses here, there was much trade with Europe. Men of courage and daring were attracted to the port, men with the spirit of adventure in their blood. Hundreds of Devon men who sailed with Drake, Raleigh, Grenville, Gilbert and Frobisher would never have been as far as Exeter in their lives, but they knew the coasts of Europe and the far off Indies as well as they knew the narrow lanes and streets of their home towns and villages. At this time the chief streets were around Sutton Pool, and were soon spreading out into Old Town. Drake had a home in Looe Street and the Hawkins lived in Kinterbury and Woolster streets. Ships were being built along the Cattewater bringing many trades to the town. Ships came in with imports of cloth, linen, iron ore and wine. Many more great expeditions sailed from Sutton Pool: Captain Cook to Australia; Captain Robert Scott to the Antarctic; Edward Wakefield with a party of settlers to New Zealand.

So Plymouth has continued as a great commercial centre right up to the present day. The three towns Plymouth, Devonport and Stonehouse were amalgamated in 1914, and Plymouth became a city in 1928. Plymouth has suffered much through wars and it has always risen, Phoenix-like, from its ashes, alert to the changing times and yet ever mindful of its great past.

I hope the pictures in this book will stimulate an interest in the city's great history.

Acknowledgements:

I am most grateful to many people who have so generously helped me in compiling this book. In particular I wish to thank Mr. S. Rendell who has given me so many details of old Plymouth; Mr. W. Best Harris; Commander L.R.R. Foster, R.N. Rtd; The Royal Western Yacht Club of England; Dr. S.R. Dennison; Mr. C.P. Dart; English China Clays; Mr. G. Little, Secretary, Plymouth Argyle Football Club; Mrs. J. Harris; The National Trust; Mrs. J. Tanner, Curator of the Cookworthy Museum, Kingsbridge; and to my husband for his splendid help.

For many of the postcards and photographs of old Plymouth I have drawn from my mother's collection, which she had formed with tremendous enthusiasm throughout the years.

GUILDHALL SQUARE, PLYMOUTH

1. A peaceful scene in Guildhall Square. With the beautiful church of St. Andrew's dominating the scene.

Union Street, Plymouth

Valentines Series 42047

2. A view of Union Street, postmarked June 1905. The policeman is on point duty. A high standing baby carriage with its large wheels stands outside the shop of the Plymouth Dairy Company, and a horse and trap outside the Florist. The hanging sign of Wright, Hair Dresser, is clearly visible. John Foulston, the architect, gave Union Street its name because it linked Plymouth with Stonehouse and Devonport.

3. Another view of Union Street, with the tram lines clearly visible. The wide pavement allowed the shop blinds to hang very low, I expect there were a few bumped heads. We can see the sign on the side of one blind, which reads Stokes & Son Ltd., Cash Chemists.

Plymouth. St Andrew's Cross.

Dear Maud. Sunday night Oct. 26 190... A sudden thought came into my head to night did I put a stamp on your letter to day I dont know if I did now but if I did not I know you will forgive...

4. A very fine photograph showing St. Andrew's Church and the old Guildhall; the card is postmarked 1902. Note the interesting ladies costumes, the policeman on point duty and the horse and cart making its leisurely progress. The cost of building the granite tower of the church was paid for by Thomas Yogge, on condition that the local people should provide the materials. The tower is 136 feet, the highest in Devon.

St. Andrew's Church and Guild Hall Square, Plymouth. Valentines Series

give my love to B P when you see him. Tell him I think he could have of come out the other...

I expect you know this

5. This picture taken in Edwardian days shows St. Andrew's Church and Guildhall Square. Note the neatly laid out garden with grass and shrubs.

6. A rare view of Plymouth, circa 1914, taken from the Citadel. The obelisk in the foreground commemorates the men who fell in the Boer War. Other well-known buildings of those days are clearly visible.

7. A remarkable view of the Post Office, what a fine building it was, standing sedately in Guildhall Square. The whole picture has a curiously continental air about it.

Mutley Plain, Plymouth

PLYMOUTH
MUTUAL
CO-OPERATIVE
SOCIETY, L⁻
BUTCHERY   BOO⁻
DAIRY   GRO⁻
DEPARTMENT

Valentine's Series

8. A scene from Mutley Plain in Edwardian days. We see the tram trundling along, an advertisement for Fry's Pure Cocoa on its side. The building of the Plymouth Mutual Co-operative and Industrial Society is clearly marked. Mutley Plain was always a busy shopping area as it is today, although the actual buildings are much changed.

9. The Guildhall and Bedford Street and the Bedford Hotel. The hackney carriages plying for hire may be seen on the left of the picture.

10. Upon this site once stood a cherry orchard. We see the magnificent façade of the Theatre Royal, designed by the eminent architect John Foulston in 1811. The theatre opened in 1813 with a performance of Shakespeare's 'As You Like It'. Throughout the nineteenth century and into the twentieth some of England's finest actors and actresses came to play upon its stage. Never a great money spinner the theatre continued until 1937, when, alas, it was demolished to make way for a cinema.

11. Another view of the Theatre Royal with Derry's Clock in the centre of the picture. One of Plymouth's most famous landmarks Derry's Clock still stands, although all around is changed, it was always a favourite meeting place. Who was Mr. Derry who gave his name to this fine edifice? William Derry was Mayor of Plymouth from 1861 to 1863, he presented the clock and almost half the cost of the tower, to the people of Plymouth. The tower stands at a height of 60 feet, and in those days it was at the very heart of the city.

PLYMOUTH. THE RESERVOIR.

BAZLEY & Co PLYMOUTH

12. The Reservoir, 1907, this was always a pleasant place to visit, quiet and peaceful, and yet almost in the centre of the busy city. Seats were provided for rest and relaxation, and with the fountains playing it was a delightful scene of tranquility and peace.

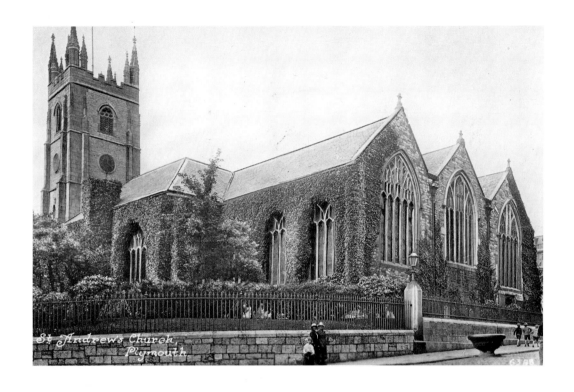

13. This is a fine photograph of St. Andrew's Church, the Mother Church of Plymouth. In the 1920's when this photograph was taken the church was ivy covered in many parts.

14. A scene at Derry's Clock, with the old tram setting down passengers. The offices of the South Western Railway are a fine block of buildings on the right of the picture.

The Old 5 horse Car at the Halfpenny Gate Plymouth.

15. The old five horse tram at Halfpenny Gate. The curious name came about when a new bridge was built across Stonehouse Pool to reach Plymouth, and named Stonehouse Bridge. The idea for the bridge was formulated by the Earl of Mount Edgecumbe and Sir John St. Aubyn. It was a good bridge, but walkers had to pay a halfpenny toll, hence its nickname, horses and carts and carriages paid up to sixpence. This irksome toll was abolished by the Plymouth Corporation on 1st April, 1921.

16. This is a very interesting postcard of an old city tram, with its open top deck, the driver, two conductors and an inspector. The electric trams came in 1899, and were a popular means of transport throughout the three towns of Stonehouse, Devonport and Plymouth.

FORE STREET, DEVONPORT.

17. Fore Street, Devonport, at the turn of the century, a busy thoroughfare with trams running down the centre, horses and carts moving at a leisurely pace. Devonport was formerly called Plymouth Dock until its name was changed by George IV in 1824, this event was commemorated by the building of the Naval Column, designed by John Foulston.

18. The wide expanse of Bedford Street, with the premises of Bateman the Optician in the centre, the enormous pair of spectacles are quite a feature. With the trams, buses, delivery vans and pedestrians, this area was often badly congested.

19. Another view of Bedford Street. In those days cars could park on either side of the street. This was a busy shopping area. Tuckett & Sons with their name on the shopblind in the foreground were a firm of manufacturing and wholesale confectioners, their factory was in Bishop's Place, West Hoe. The premises seen here at 56, Bedford Street was their retail shop.

The Marine Biological Laboratory, The Hoe, Plymouth.

20. A splendid view of the Marine Biological Laboratory, this card is postmarked 1903. It also houses a delightful Aquarium, which I well remember being taken to visit on wet days. The Laboratory is well-known throughout the world for its scientific research.

VIEW FROM SMEATON TOWER, PLYMOUTH

21. This photograph taken from Smeaton Tower shows the magnificent setting of the Marine Biological Laboratory, with the walls of the Citadel beyond and the curving road leading down to the Barbican, now one-way only. The headquarters of the Mayflower Sailing Club may be glimpsed below the Citadel.

View from Smeaton Tower, Plymouth Hoe.

JWS 220

22. An unusual view taken from Smeaton Tower. Drake's Island is prominent in the background, formerly called St. Nicolas's Island it acquired its present name after Sir Francis Drake's father took his family to live there after leaving their home near Tavistock. A chapel once stood on the rocks of the island, it was also used as a prison, and Cromwell's general, John Lambert, died there in 1683. Today the rugged six acres provide an adventure training centre for the young.

Hoe Pier, Plymouth

23. A tranquil scene in Edwardian days of the Hoe Pier, the view is taken from the West Hoe.

THE HOE SLOPES PLYMOUTH

24. The Hoe Slopes, postmarked 1907. Smeaton Tower and the bandstand dominate the skyline. The Belvedere on the right of the picture was a welcome refuge when the winds were blowing in from the English Channel, it serves the same purpose today. Note the sailor hurrying down the path in the foreground, not many sailors in uniform are seen about in Plymouth today, since they are permitted to wear mufti when off-duty.

Plymouth. Dear Maud The Pier.

my first card I hope will find you much better, I feel awfully sorry to hear of your misfortune, am writing to morrow. Yours C.

25. A pleasing scene of the Pier and the Sound as it must have looked in 1902, when this card was posted. As today, there is plenty of activity in the Sound with yachts and boats of every description, including sailing barges, and two and three-masted schooners.

ARBICAN FISH QUAY PLYMOUTH.

26. The Barbican Fish Quay, circa 1908. It stands at the head of Sutton Pool, and here we see the fishermen scrubbing down their nets, with the fishing boats at anchor. A fine fishing fleet sailed from here in good weather and bad, a welcome sight to see them coming into harbour with their red and brown and lemon sails, the boats laden with catches to be despatched all over the country.

27. A picture of the last wooden schooner to trade from the West Country. The Kathleen and May was launched in 1900, her cargo capacity was 240 tons, and her sail area 6,400 square feet. The crew was a master, a mate and four seamen. We see this fine old schooner as she looked after being restored by the Maritime Trust, and moored in Sutton Pool, with the Barbican in the background.

28. Old Town Street as it used to look. There was always much activity here, with a meat market in the centre and a leather hall above it. Carriages once ran regular services from here to Plymouth Dock, the fare was one shilling. The area was also known for its breweries, supplying the numerous inns existing here in the nineteenth and the early part of the twentieth century.

29. A close-up view of the Pier. Note the advertisement for the Masquerade Follies. Concert parties were a regular part of the entertainment provided, and much patronised on wet days. The café with its sea views was also very popular.

Plymouth.

Drake's Statue and Promenade.

Oh what a lovely place wished you
could have come Its cleared

30. The Hoe Promenade with Drake's statue surveying the scene. The pleasing façade of Elliot Terrace may be seen on the right of the picture, No. 3 was the home of Lord and Lady Astor for many years. Of particular interest is the dress of the lady wearing the long gown and cape, with the small child in white dress and straw hat, circa 1903.

Plymouth. The Hoe and Drake's Statue.

Dear Maud. Every thing here is "all Quiff" D.P.

31. A closer view on the Hoe of Drake's statue, and the graceful houses beyond. Fortunately Elliot Terrace still stands, but the building next to it, once the headquarters of the Royal Western Yacht Club of England, has gone. This card is postmarked 20th August 1903 and bears the familiar Plymouth stamp 620 in horizontal lines, this mark was shortly to disappear for ever.

32. This superb view from Plymouth Hoe shows the West Hoe Swimming Baths 1870.
Today it is the Royal Western Yacht Club of England. A worthy setting for the famous
club who have organised many events, such as the Single-handed Transatlantic Races, the
Fastnet Race, and exciting round-the-world events that have captured the imagination of
thousands world-wide.

30832. PLYMOUTH: WEST HOE & PIER.

33. The West Hoe and the Royal Western Yacht Club of England on the right of the picture, circa 1920. A pleasure steamer is coming in to the promenade Pier.

PLYMOUTH HOE FROM PIER

34. This would have been a familiar scene to many people. Photographed from the Pier, and postmarked 1921.

Hoe Pier and Drake's Island, Plymouth.

35. Another good view of the Hoe Pier, showing the domes and ornate ironwork, the pier was built in 1884, and was a favourite rendez-vous for townspeople and visitors. This card is dated 1904 and bears the Plymouth postmark.

36. Here we see an amazing picture of the rough sea at West Hoe in April, 1922. The Royal South Western Yacht Club premises suffered severe damage, the sea in all its fury rushed in at one door and out of another, but the building withstood the onslaught.

String Band of H.M. Royal Marines.

(PLYMOUTH DIVISION)

By kind permission of Brigadier G. CARPENTER, O.B.E., D.S.C., and Officers, Royal Marines.

Programme of Music.

1.—MARCH	..	" Nautical Moments "	.. ..	*Winter*
2.—SUITE	..	" On the Briny "	.. ..	*Carr*
3.—SELECTION ..	..	" Iolanthe "	.. .. ..	*Sullivan*
4.—TWO DANCES		(a) " Liebesfrued " ..	.. ..	*Kriesler*
		(b) " Liebeslied "		
5.—THREE FRIVOLITIES	.. .. ..		.. ..	*Fletcher*
6.—SELECTION	..	" Five o'Clock Girl " ..	.. ..	*Ruby*
7.—VALSE		" Beautiful Blue Danube "	.. ..	*Strauss*
8.—SELECTION	..	" Blue Eyes "	.. .. ..	*Kern*
9.—PATROL	..	" The Pixies "	.. .. ..	*Trotere*
10.—SELECTION	.. ..	" Show Boat "	.. ..	*Kern*

Royal South Western Yacht Club.

❧❧❧

ANNUAL REGATTA

—— Thursday, July 24th, 1930. ——

❧❧❧

Commodore :
K. EYTON PECK, ESQ.

Vice-Commodore :
M. E. NEGUS, ESQ.

Rear-Commodore :
J. E. S. LONG, ESQ.

Hon. Treasurer ;
A. R. WHITMARSH, ESQ.

Hon. Secretary :
D. M. MURDOCH, ESQ.

---

37. The annual Regatta of the Royal Western Yacht Club is always the high spot of the sailing year. The year 1930 was no exception, it had many distinguished yachtsmen competing, including T.O.M. Sopwith, in the Yachts of the 12-Metre Class with his yacht 'Mouette', also the Rt. Hon. The Earl of Essex with his yacht 'Rhona', and C.R. Fairey sailing 'Flica'. The String Band of H.M. Royal Marines (Plymouth Division) played a lively programme of music.

284

Plymouth. Eddystone Lighthouse. *October 19ᵗʰ 1902.*

Yours &c Charlie

Dear Maud,
Another for your collection
Your trip to Combe, said Mr White Saturday
so sorry to hear of Annie's disappointment
must reserve a day during November as
suggested, I hope your hand is getting Better

38. Known to every mariner who sails the English Channel, the Eddystone Lighthouse sends out its warning light. Built on a rocky reef where the tides swirl and whirl above the treacherous rocks below. This lighthouse took four years to build, 1878 to 1882, the stump of the former Eddystone Light may be seen behind it, this was Smeaton's Tower, the upper part was removed and now stands on Plymouth Hoe. It was the constant wearing away of the rock that made the new lighthouse a necessity, it was built upon a larger rock and at a lower level.

39. From 1842 to 1878 this was the Club House of the Royal South Western Yacht Club. The building was known as Mr. Clouter's House, it stood at the corner of Hobart Street and Buckingham Place, Stonehouse.

Plymouth. The Hoe Promenade.

apl. 22nd 1903

Congratulations on your birthday W. Hazelgrove Searle

40. Looking across the wide expanse of the Hoe in 1903. It shows Smeaton's Tower, Drake's statue, the Armada Memorial and the Citadel, with the distinctive building of the Marine Biological Laboratory. This view was sent as a birthday card to my mother.

41. A splendid photograph of the training ship H.M.S. Impregnable in the Hamoaze. A training ship for young sailors for many years, this scene is particularly interesting as it shows the ship with a wreath up for an officers wedding.

42. This is the beautiful Elizabethan House now restored to its former glory. Situated in New Street, one of the oldest streets in the Barbican area, this house was in a sorry state when it was rescued from demolition by the endeavours of the Old Plymouth Society. Today the house is furnished with solid pieces of furniture from Elizabethan days, the small diamond panes of glass glint in the sunlight throwing patterns across the old wooden floors within.

43. Also in New Street and directly opposite the Elizabethan House we see another house of the same period. This picture shows the solid stone walling of the adjoining building. The street is narrow, and the houses appear to lean towards each other. It is exciting to realise that our great sailors of the past, Drake, Hawkins, Raleigh, Grenville, Frobisher and Gilbert, along with many others must have walked this narrow street, and would certainly have known these houses as they look today.

Armada Monument, Plymouth

44. The impressive Armada Memorial on Plymouth Hoe. The foundation stone was laid in 1888, the year of the tercentenary celebrations. The amazing triumph of the English fleet in July 1588 under their Admiral, Lord Howard of Effingham in the Ark Royal, and his Vice-Admiral Francis Drake on the Revenge is history, written in prose and poetry, a proud day to remember.

ARMADA MEMORIAL. PLYMOUTH HOE

D.F & C? York.

45. This peaceful scene of the Armada Memorial was taken by moonlight, circa 1905.

BANDSTAND & SMEATON TOWN, PLYMOUTH

46. A lively crowd on Plymouth Hoe in Edwardian days. The regular band concerts held there were very popular as we see from the animated throng. Others are enjoying the scene from the viewing balcony on Smeaton Tower.

Plymouth Hoe

47. Another view of the Hoe sent from Plymouth in 1904. Plenty of room for the crowds who flocked here for a pleasant walk or to sit around the bandstand and listen to the music. We can see the Citadel with the gun emplacements clearly visible, also Smeaton's Lighthouse brought from the Eddystone Reef and re-erected on the Hoe in 1884, a solid structure, well designed, its flashing light warned mariners of the treacherous rocks around its base for over 123 years. It was built by John Smeaton, the Yorkshire engineer, and had it not been undermined by the crumbling rocks below it would probably be out on the Eddystone Reef flashing still.

THE NEW "MAYFLOWER" MEMORIAL
STONE AND TABLET, BARBICAN, PLYMOUTH

On the 6 of September 1620, in the Mayoralty of Thomas Townes after being kindly entertained and courteously used by divers Friends there dwelling, the Pilgrim Fathers sailed from Plymouth in the Mayflower in the Providence of God to settle in NEW PLYMOUTH and to lay the Foundation of the NEW ENGLAND STATES. ～ The ancient Causey whence they embarked was destroyed not many Years afterwards, but the Site of their Embarkation is marked by the Stone bearing the name of the MAYFLOWER in the pavement of the adjacent Pier. This Tablet was erected in the Mayoralty of J. T. Bond 1891 to commemorate their Departure and the visit to Plymouth in July of that Year of a number of their Descendants and Representatives.

48. A place of pilgrimage for thousands from the old world and the new. A visit to the Mayflower Memorial is a must. This simple stone and tablet marks the spot from whence the Pilgrim Fathers set sail from Old Sutton Pool Quay on the Barbican, for America. The date was 6th September 1620, six weeks later than they had planned, thus they ran into the winter Atlantic gales. The Mayflower was built in the early part of the seventeenth century, and she weighed 180 tons, there were no portholes, and the height between decks was four feet nine inches, many of the passengers did not survive the exhausting journey of 67 days.

49. This plaque on the wall of the Island House on the Barbican recalls the names of some of the pilgrims who sailed from Plymouth on 6th September 1620. It had taken this group three years to obtain permission to settle in America. Finally the Mayflower set sail from Delfshaven, reaching Southampton on 19th July, she was joined here by other pilgrims from many parts of England. The Speedwell, the groups second vessel, arrived a week later, but she was leaking badly, and after sailing on 5th August they had to put in to Dartmouth for repairs. Still the Speedwell leaked, and they put in at Plymouth. Considered unseaworthy for the Atlantic crossing the Speedwell returned to London. Those who finally sailed from Plymouth said they were kindly received when they stayed at the Island House. They reached Cape Cod on 9th November, the first to step ashore was John Alden from Harwich.

The Citadel Gate, Plymouth.

50. An imposing view of the Citadel Gate, this was the main gate to this impressive fortress built by Charles II for the defence of Plymouth. The architect was Sir Bernard de Gomme, the walls and buildings are of limestone and granite. The ramparts command magnificent views, especially across the Hoe and beyond. Today they may be visited at certain hours.

Boer war Memorial. Plymouth. Hoe

51. The Boer War Memorial, circa 1910, with a fine panorama of Plymouth beyond. A favoured place to visit to 'take the air'.

52. The Royal Naval Barracks, Devonport, circa 1906. These massive granite buildings were an impressive sight, built by the renowned engineer John Jackson between 1898 and 1903. Before these buildings were completed the sailors lived on a number of old hulks in the Hamoaze.

53. The Park, Devonport, at the turn of the century. It shows the ornate fountain in the foreground, with the bandstand behind. Devonport had many charming Georgian houses, some of them may be seen in the background.

54. This splendid vista taken at West Hoe shows the Grand Hotel, now Berni's, with the headquarters of the Royal Western Yacht Club on the hotel's right. Today the latter building has gone, it is just an open space, for the entire headquarters were destroyed by fire, together with many precious records. In the foreground is the picturesque Belvedere, built in 1891.

W 206   NAVAL WAR MEMORIAL, THE HOE, PLYMOUTH

55. The impressive Naval War Memorial on the Hoe, erected after the First World War. It bears the names of personnel who died, or who were killed in action.

56. A street tea party near Plymouth for a Queen Victoria Jubilee celebration. The costumes are of great interest, the beautiful lace collar of the girl in the forefront, the hats of the men, flowered hats and boaters of the women, and little boys in their sailor suits.

57. An interesting photograph of a sailor of the nineteenth century, possibly on a Devonport based ship. He had gone to John Hodge, the photographer of 31, Union Street, Stonehouse, to have his portrait taken. Note the setting of plants and ferns indicating far away places.

58. A happy beach scene taken at Mountbatten beach in July 1914. A popular place for picnics. The little girl in the foreground wears a broderie anglais dress and hat, a delightful cotton material, very cool to wear and much favoured for children's chlothes of those days; she also wears bar sandals, similar to those worn today.

PLYM BRIDGE, PLYMOUTH.

This is not Fingle Bridge, but Plym Bridge
Bickleigh Vale. Plymouth. — Lord Von Motley.

59. Plym Bridge 1901. A very beautiful place to visit at any season of the year. Around this area, and even within the city boundaries are many old farms and holdings supplying fresh fruit and vegetables for the city throughout the year. It was from this river that Plymouth took its name.

Plymouth. Saltash Bridge. *Dear Maud.* *October 22nd 1902.*

One more to the collection, dont you think it a pretty view Devonport Elevation to day and Bridgeway on both Side

60. Saltash Bridge, one of the finest constructions built by Isambard Kingdom Brunel. It was opened in 1859 as the Royal Albert Bridge by Prince Albert on 2nd May, but it has always been known as the Saltash Bridge. It crosses the tidal river Tamar and has 19 arches, the two largest are each 455 feet in length. The single railway line was laid on the broad gauge of 7 feet but was later converted to the standard gauge of 4 feet 8½ inches, between the 20th and 23rd of May 1892. It is interesting to note that Brunel's maternal grandfather was at one time Army and Land Agent at Plymouth.

SALTASH BRIDGE.

61. Another view of Saltash Bridge, with the train crossing. A triumph of engineering, this graceful bridge built by Brunel is one of his finest achievements in the West Country, it was his last completed work; sadly he was unable to be present at the opening ceremony by the Prince Consort having been very ill. He was, however, able to view the scene as he lay upon a mattress in a railway truck, he died the following September.

62. Saltash Bridge circa 1920, with the steam ferry boats alongside. The old car is waiting to make the crossing.

The "Empress." (Saltash, Three Towns, and District Steamboat Co. Ltd.)

63. A splendid picture of the steamship 'Empress', circa 1906, owned by the Saltash, Three Towns and District Steamship Co. Ltd. As we see here it was crowded with sightseers, the paddle steamer was a popular way of viewing the warships at anchor in Devonport Dockyard, and then going up the river Tamar, visiting some of the small villages on its banks, with the beautiful scenery of Devon on one side and of Cornwall on the other. The river Tamar is one of the most interesting rivers in the West Country.

64. The Royal Hotel, one of John Foulston's finest designs, with its four Ionic pillars. Derry's Clock is in the background. All the traffic is horse-drawn.

65. Looking along Bedford Street at the turn of the century. A busy thoroughfare with many fine buildings of varying designs of architecture. The unusual wrought iron lamp standard in the foreground is of particular interest.

Burrator Reservoir. *Plymouth.*

66. Burrator Reservoir situated on the edge of Dartmoor, near Sheeps Tor. When the open leat on the moor froze over in 1881 and residents of Plymouth were short of water in the depth of winter, it became urgent that another supply was available. Many sites were discussed, and Burrator was finally decided upon, it was supplying water by 1898. It was not until 1914 when the towns amalgamated that Burrator also supplied Devonport, until that time the latter town had its own leat from the West Dart river, this fed storage reservoirs at Crownhill and Stoke.

Burrator Reservoir.

67. Another view of Burrator Reservoir. This card is postmarked 'Plymouth, August 2. 1904', the writer says he arrived about 10.12 p.m. and the train was 'packed all the way down, in fact stood all the way'. This area is a favourite drive from Plymouth, and a splendid place for picnics, as may be seen by the beautiful moorland scenery.

68. A panorama of the Hoe, postmarked 'Plymouth, No. 15, 1902', and with the oval 620 mark. We see the Pier and the tower, and as always shipping in the Sound. Strolling on one of the finest promenades in Europe was as popular then as it is today.

69. Plymouth Hoe from another angle, the card is postmarked 1912. The view is taken from the Citadel looking towards Drake's Island with the wooded slopes of Mount Edgecumbe in the distance.

MOUNT WISE, DEVONPORT.

70. Mount Wise, Devonport, circa 1905, with the signal station at the top of the picture. The pleasant residence in the foreground is not what it seems, for it was the Royal Clarence Baths, in the early nineteenth century they had vapour, shower and swimming baths, hot and cold; at the back of the building was a small beach. We can see the Admiral's boathouse and Bullock Dock. The Dock was turned into public swimming baths in 1924.

71. A portrait of Mr. Arthur Benstead, the author's uncle. He was a schoolmaster in Stonehouse from 1904, remaining there for many years, until he was appointed headmaster at Withycombe Raleigh School, there he remained until his retirement.

Mount Edgcumbe House from the Avenue

72. The magnificent Mount Edgecumbe House, seen from the Avenue. With its Gothic front and beautiful park it is a lovely place to visit. This is where Turner painted a great deal of his 'Crossing the Brook' picture. Reached by the Cremyll ferry the view is one of centuries past. Today you can wander at will in the many acres of varied scenery, including ten miles of coastline. The gardens were landscaped in the eighteenth century, with an orangery, an Italian garden, a French garden, a jet d'eau and an amphitheatre.

73. The Rt. Hon. the Earl of Mount Edgecumbe
(1833-1917) was the 4th Earl. At the time this
photograph was taken he was the Commodore
of the Royal South Western Yacht Club, 1901.
The original portrait hangs in the club lounge.

BEECHWOOD COTTAGE, MOUNT EDGECUMBE, NEAR PLYMOUTH.

74. A charming pastoral scene of Beechwood Cottage on the Mount Edgecumbe estate. Note the picnic party in the foreground. This photograph was taken in Edwardian days.

Plymouth. View from Mount Edgcumbe. *Dear M.* *October 24 1902.*
forgive a letter this week, will write on Sunday when I
have great news concerning my welfare. Yours until then

75. An idylic cameo taken from the eighteenth century folly, known as the Ruin, on the Mount Edgcumbe estate. Below the folly are the hanging woods above Barn Pool, with Drake's Island and Plymouth beyond.

Plymouth Argyle 1903-1904

Standing : W. ANDERSON   H. WINTERHOLDER   C. CLARK   F. FITCHETT   J. ROBINSON   A. CLARK   J. BANKS   J. PICKEN   B. JACK

Seated :   T. CLEGHORN   B. DALYRMPLE   W. LEECH   A. GOODHALL   J. PEDDIE   H. DIGWEED   F. BRETTELL

76. A fine photograph of the Plymouth Argyle Football Team, 1903-04, the first season the club had become professional. They quickly built up a reputation as doughty cup fighters. They did well in qualifying rounds and were drawn against the First Division Champions, Sheffield Wednesday, in the first round. A crowd of over 20,000 watched the match at Home Park, which resulted in a draw 2-2. They went down in the replay at Hillsborough by two goals.

ARGYLE v. NEWCASTLE. February, 1905.

Charles & Co., Devonport.

77. This is a rare photograph taken at the Argyle v Newcastle cup tie replay match at Home Park, 8th February 1905, the Argyle team are in the dark (green) jerseys, the result of the match was a 1-1 draw. The Argyle team had defeated Barnsley in the qualifying round, and were then drawn away to the First Division leaders, the mighty Newcastle United. During the week prior to the game, the team received arduous training at Newbiggin-on-Sea. Great interest was aroused in Plymouth, and an excursion was arranged in the Devonport Dockyard. The football world was amazed when Plymouth Argyle drew once again 1-1, the goalscorer was Picken, and the gate was 28,000. Newcastle United came to Plymouth as we see in the photo above, the gate was 17,000 and the goalscorer was Buck. The second replay was held at Plumstead when Argyle lost by two goals to nil.

78. The name of Robert Jack is a legend to Plymouth Argyle Football Club. The first professional player to sign for Argyle he was a great sportsman in every way. His home town was Alloa, Scotland, he played for Alloa Athletic when only fifteen years of age, and also played for Fifeshire. He was signed by Bolton Wanderers and played six seasons for them, gaining a reputation as one of the fastest wingers in the country. Robert Jack came to Argyle in 1903, and in 1905 he was appointed player-manager, when the then manager Mr. Frank Brettell joined the Board. It is interesting to note that in Alloa he was articled for four years to a local solicitor, and during this time was the organist at the Established Church. Leaving Argyle for a brief spell with Southend United as secretary and player, until in 1910 he answered an S.O.S. from Argyle and returned as their manager. His proud association with the club was unbroken until he retired in 1938.

79. A great sportsman, John W. Sutcliffe joined Plymouth Argyle as goalkeeper in 1904, and remained at Home Park until 1912. He was a Yorkshireman who had played for England under both the Rugby and Soccer codes. Before coming to Plymouth he played for Bolton Wanderers, Millwall and Manchester United. He played five games as goalkeeper for England, 1893 versus Wales; 1895 versus Scotland; 1895 versus Ireland; 1901 versus Scotland and 1903 versus Wales. His Rugby cap for England came in the season 1888-89, when he played against the Maoris. At that time he was playing for the Heckmondwike R.U. Club. Standing 6 feet in height and weighing 13½ stone he was a powerful player.

F. M. WATERS
& Co.

4 TO NIL!

We wish to draw your attention to the fact that the Points .. .. Scored for our

21/-, 25/- and 30/- OVERCOATS

—ARE FOR—

1—FIT.
2—FINISH.
3—VALUE.
4—VARIETY.

MARKET PLACE, PLYMOUTH.

80. Old advertisements are always fascinating, and here we have one issued by F.M. Waters & Co. of Market Place, Plymouth, they were located between G.P. Holmes, house furnishers and drapers, and F.L. Knight the tailor. The football jargon used in the advertisement is particularly striking and must have brought in many customers.

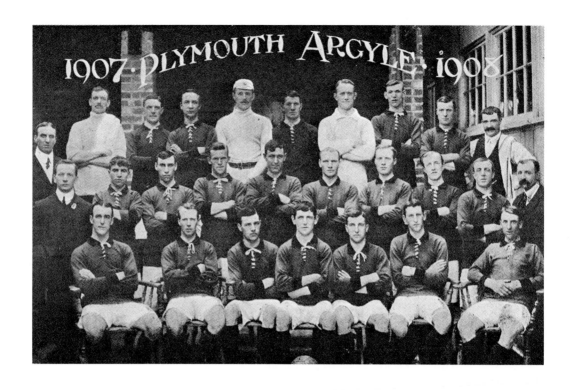

81. A striking photograph of the Plymouth Argyle Football Team 1907-08. Older Residents will recognise many familiar faces. This was the season in which a new Committee of Management was formed amongst the directors, with Mr. Louis Crabb as secretary.

82. W.J. Baker, known as Billy, was a handsome
Plymouth-born footballer. He became a
member of the Argyle team in 1909 from the
local team Green Waves. He made no less than
197 appearances for the Argyle first team. He
joined the army in 1915 and was killed in
action in France in 1917. He was awarded the
D.C.M.

83. Harry Raymond was a popular member of the Argyle team. He was born at Crownhill, and was one of the most brilliant of the local lads who joined in 1909. He played for England in international matches against Wales, Ireland and Holland in 1914. It is interesting to note that the first of these games was played at Home Park, and the English side included such famous players as A.E. Knight, Ivan Sharpe and Vivian Woodward; one of England's goals was scored by Harry.

NICHOLS'

The Greatest House
for
Football
and all Sports. .. ..

Endless Variety.

Magnificent Display .. No need to go elsewhere

FOOTBALLS, 5/6 to 12/6.

FOOTBALL BOOTS, 3/11 to 12/8.

KNICKERS, 1/-, 1/6, 1/9, 2/-.

SHIRTS AND JERSEYS, FROM

.. .. 21/- per dozen. .. ..

NICHOLS & Co.,
TELEPHONE No. 605.

LIMITED. **Illustrated Catalogue Free.**

148, UNION ST., PLYMOUTH.

84. A lively advertisement from 1910 came from Nichols' the Sports Outfitters of 148 Union Street, Plymouth. The prices speak for themselves.

85. Here we see Tom Watts, the jovial host of the Prince of Wales Inn, Saltash Road, Morice Town, Devonport. This photograph was taken circa 1907. The inn was close to the Naval Dockyard and would no doubt have had many naval personnel and dock workers as its clients, as well as being the 'local' for the many residents living nearby. In those days a 4½ gallon cask of outmeal stout could be purchased for 5/3d, and a dozen pints in bottles for 2/6d.

Prince of Wales Inn,
Wine and Spirit Vaults, Morice Town.

Ale and Porter drawn from the Wood.
Tom Watts, Opposite Keyham Gates.

86. George Street, a busy business area as it looked circa 1900. At one time there were two foundries here, one of them being Mare's Foundry, who built the Hearless Patent Fire Engine, also a great deal of machinery for the ships entering the port in increasing numbers every year. The machinery for the floating bridge at Dartmouth was built here.

87. A remarkable photograph of a tailor and his apprentices. The young men each hold a different tool, a needle and thread, a measure, and the centre apprentice is using a large pressing iron, this is being passed across a sleeve board. Yards of material cover their knees.

THE LIDO, PLYMOUTH

88. A summer scene from the 1920's taken at the Lido. A highly popular place for swimming and sunbathing as the card shows.

Ivybridge, Devon.

JWS 217

89. A typical Dartmoor scene at Ivybridge 1905. This pleasant area of the Erme Valley was much favoured by the people of Plymouth, being cool and sparkling on hot days, and not far from the city. The river runs down from Dartmoor over great granite boulders and is a place of great beauty.

90. A delightful landscaped park provides the setting for a remarkable survival of a George II mansion, Saltram House, with its original contents on display. Only 3½ miles from Plymouth city centre this fine house, once the home of the Parker family, is now open to the public by the National Trust. This view shows the west front from the Lime Walk.

91. The exquisite dining-room of Saltram House, restored to its pristine beauty, as it was designed by Robert Adam. Note the beautiful plaster ceilings. There are pictures by Sir Joshua Reynolds who was born nearby at Plympton Erle, the son of Samuel Reynolds, a clergyman, and headmaster of Plympton Grammar School, which his son attended.

92. The Morning Room at Saltram House, the furniture epitomizes the taste of the late eighteenth century, with the Chinese Chippendale chairs and the beautiful black and gold lacquer cabinet in the background. Again we see paintings by Sir Joshua Reynolds, his pictures of children have a special tenderness and beauty which have given world-wide appreciation to his works. After his father died he returned to Plymouth in 1747 and lived in Plymouth Dock, now Devonport.

93. The Saloon at Saltram House, one of the most important rooms designed by Robert Adam. Fine period furniture delights the eye, china and pictures have been delightfully grouped, and the soft colourings must be seen to be truly appreciated.

94. The Chinese Bedroom at Saltram House shows the great Chinese influence of the period, even to the wallpaper, and the pieces of porcelain on the mantelpiece. What a joy it is to see this beautiful room, just as it must have looked when it was first created.

95. The Chinese Dressing Room, full of reminders of the past. The hip bath placed in front of the wrought iron fireplace, the footbath and the brown enamel hot water cans, and what looks like a tablet of Pear's soap in its dish, these stand on a blue and white rag rug, made of cotton and easy to wash. Note the small mahogany washstand with petite jug and basin. The towel rail in the corner will be remembered by many people. Encompassing it all is the delightful Chinese wallpaper.

96. The kitchen at Saltram House as it must have looked in Victorian and Edwardian days. The fine utensils used at that time have been carefully gathered together, the scrubbed tables, white mixing bowls, the sets of polished copper saucepans and other utensils hanging in the corner. The glowing fire with the kettle ready for cook's cup of tea.

Church Street,

What day are you coming home?

South Brent

E 16633

97. A rural scene in South Brent, 1905. The costumes of the onlookers are of particular interest.

The Railway Station.

This is were I have to run to catch the train every morn...

South Brent.

E. 16635

98. The Railway Station, South Brent, circa 1905, is typical of so many country stations of those days, with the connecting bridge for the up and down trains. Note the ticket office and the waiting rooms, giving plenty of shelter during the winter months. A beautiful stretch of Dartmoor may be seen in the background.

Fore Street, South Brent. E 16634

Hope you are not working too hard.

99. Fore Street, South Brent, circa 1905, the shop of Hosking and the Angel Hotel. Several of the little girls wear the wide shouldered pinafores of the day. The photographer is evidently causing a great deal of interest.

100. A peaceful scene of Fore Street, Kingsbridge, postmarked 1905. Still a quiet country town, and yet so near to Plymouth. On the picturesque quay coastal vessels would unload, and reload with the wool manufactured here. Later the town became a busy market centre for the fertile agricultural area around.

No 1. Garden Front of School House

101. This postcard shows the garden front of the old Kingsbridge Grammar School, where it is reputed William Cookworthy attended. It is now the Cookworthy Museum with many interesting details of his life, they are housed in the old schoolroom, with its original panelling and inscribed with generations of schoolboys initials. Several rare examples of the porcelain Cookworthy made at Plymouth are on view.

102. This is the famous portrait of William Cookworthy, the founder of the English China Clay industry. It was painted by John Opie R.A. at Cookworthy's home in Notte Street, Plymouth. At that time it was one of the finest houses of the Queen Anne period, the front was built of Portland stone. There was a garden with William's chemical laboratory on one side. There are few portraits of this remarkable man who left his home in Kingsbridge to walk to London at the age of 15 years, to work at the laboratory of Silvanus Bevan, who had met the lad whilst visiting the town, was struck by his intelligence and offered to take him into business, he prepared medicines of mineral origin.

103. Here we see two exquisite pieces of porcelain, manufactured by William Cookworthy at his Coxside factory at Plymouth. At the age of 21 Cookworthy had come to Plymouth with Silvanus Bevan as his partner, to set up a business as manufacturing chemists. Bevan was a Fellow of the Royal Society, a very informed scientist. In his spare hours William had taught himself French and Latin. Both Quakers they worked hard and long in their business. William was also a Minister of the Society of Friends and this took him on horseback into many parts of Cornwall, as he rode he studied the geology of the county.

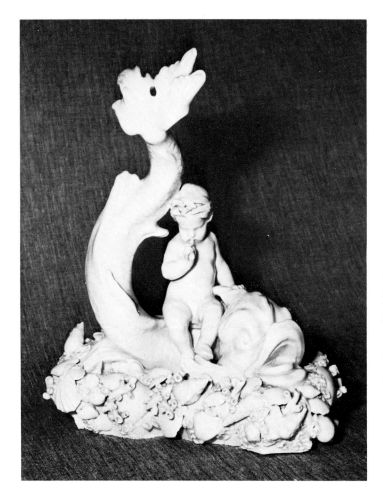

104. Another beautiful piece of William Cookworthy's porcelain in the pure white glaze which he developed. His interest in ceramics was no doubt stimulated by pieces brought to Plymouth on his brother's ship, sailing from China. He made many experiments with the clay he found near St. Austell, Cornwall, in the parish of St. Stephens. He discovered that the clays used in China came from the Kaolin Hills, outside Peking, and that the clay he had found in Cornwall produced an even whiter body. That was the most exciting event in the history of English porcelain, now for the first time, true, hard paste, fluorescent porcelain was being produced, and in Plymouth.

105. William Cookworthy had obtained a patent for his discovery, and Plymouth porcelain was well established. At one time a Frenchman called Soqui was employed, a fine artist in painting exotic birds, he had worked at the Sèvres factory in France. The two birds illustrated, painted in varied bright colours are probably some of his work.

106. The Royal William Victualling Yard from Mount Wise, Devonport. It was designed by Sir John Rennie, a huge severe piece of architecture in an imposing waterfront setting, mostly three fine blocks of limestone ashlar with local granite facings. The entrance gateway with carved granite anchors, oxheads and rope showing the functions of the yard.

107. This charming scene of the Swiss Lodge and Gardens in Devonport Park shows how
it must have looked circa 1885. Swiss style lodges and chalets were very popular at this
time, following the fashion set by Queen Victoria with her charming Swiss Chalet in the
grounds of Osborne House on the Isle of Wight.

108. The Citadel circa 1885, a formidable fort built for the defence of Plymouth by Charles II. The King paid many visits during construction, he had requisitioned houses and land and took a great interest in the whole design. At one time he stayed in the Citadel with his brother James when he came to inspect the Hamoaze and the Cattewater. It is still one of the most impressive fortifications in the country. Today it is the home of 29 Commando Regiment Royal Artillery. The small and beautiful chapel of St. Katherine is within the fort.

109. The Raglan Barracks, Devonport, were built at a time when there were several new fortifications in and around Plymouth. The year was 1854, and the barracks were called after the Commander in the Crimean War, Field-Marshal Lord Raglan. He was the first British general who had to conduct operations in the field whilst being advised, controlled, directed, and censured by telegraphic despatches from the War Office. With patient courage he fulfilled his office to the last, and won devotion from all ranks serving under him.

110. The entrance to the Royal Marine Barracks, Stonehouse, in the late nineteenth century. We see the Commandant's house and staff quarters. When an extension was made the railings were taken down. The building was a stone fronted Palladian design.

111. Mount Wise, circa 1880. A number of visitors are looking on at the parade ceremony. Prince Alfred Duke of Edinburgh lived here when he was Naval Commander-in-Chief, with him was his daughter Princess Marie, who became Queen Marie of Rumania. On 31st May 1924 Queen Marie visited Plymouth and was presented with a scroll from the Corporation, together with a commemorative gold casket. This casket is now in the Museum of Rumanian History, Bucharest.

112. The Royal Albert Bridge, circa 1880. This is of particular interest because we see the steam ferry about to make the crossing to Saltash. There is a great deal of activity on both banks of the Tamar.

113. H.M.S. Impregnable moored in the Hamoaze, circa 1880. This was the well-known training ship for sailor boys.

114. The entrance to the Dockyard, Devonport, circa 1880. The town of Dock had grown with amazing speed around the Naval Yard and men flocked from all parts of the country to work here. The town grew, and some fine buildings were designed by John Foulston, the first was the Town Hall, situated at the top of Ker Street. The inhabitants were proud of their town, and in 1823 they sent a petition to King George IV for permission to change its name. The King gave it the name of Devonport, and this was first used in 1824.

115. This dignified entrance to Keyham Steam Yard, Morice Town, Devonport is very imposing, circa 1880. It was designed by the London born architect Sir Charles Barry, who had won the design for the new Houses of Parliament in public competition.

116. The Municipal Buildings as they appeared in 1876. The carriage and pair making leisurely progress, the crinolined ladies and bowler hatted gentlemen set the scene from another age.

117. A view of the Breakwater and Staddon Heights from the Hoe. The Breakwater was completed in 1842, John Rennie was the architect. Four million tons of limestone and three million tons of granite facing blocks were used in the construction. The Breakwater is over a mile in length, its cost was one and a half million pounds, and its value to shipping has been immensurable.

118. One of the finest architectural views of old Plymouth. John Foulston was an architect of remarkable vision, his Royal Hotel and Assembly Rooms, coupled with his Theatre Royal were some of his greatest achievements. John Foulston settled in Plymouth after winning the competition for the design of the Royal Hotel, and from then on became the principal town planner and architect.

119. The Garrison, Catwater and Battery, circa 1880. At this time Catwater, now spelt Cattewater, was busy with ships from many parts of the world, and several shipbuilders had their yards here.

120. The Gothic frontage of the Duke of Cornwall Hotel, a very highclass hotel of the nineteenth century. Fortunately it still stands and is even more popular today, having been fully modernised and well equipped for modern living, whilst retaining its nineteenth century charm.

121. Sherwell Chapel circa 1880. It was built in 1864 and served an expanding population of Congregationalists in the area. The first minister at Sherwell was Charles Wilson who was there from 1864 to 1882, he had previously been at Norley Chapel which closed for two years after Sherwell was opened.

122. A nineteenth century view of the old Guildhall, a massive building, it replaced the
earlier Jacobean Guildhall of 1606. Opened in 1874 by H.R.H. The Prince of Wales it
contained a courtroom and a prison, with a market on the ground floor.

123. The Prince of Wales Redoubt at Stonehouse Point was a strong fort as we see from the picture.

124. A pleasing scene of Laira Bridge, circa 1876. The construction of this iron bridge over the Laira Estuary in 1827 by James Rendell, (he was then only 25 years of age) greatly eased the route to Plymstock. Travellers had previously had to rely on small ferry services. When the bridge was built it was the second longest iron bridge in the country.

125. The Park, Devonport, circa 1880. A fountain plays as the inhabitants stroll along the wide paths, with a fine view of the passing shipping.

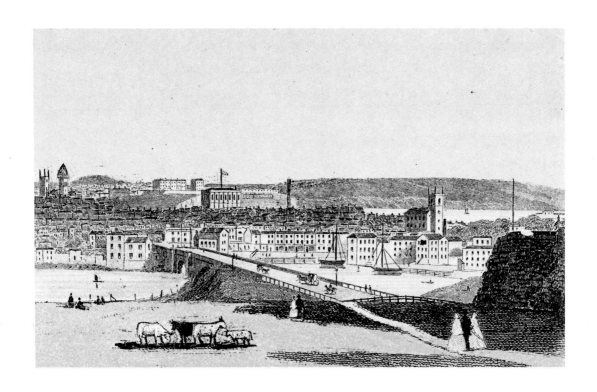

126. Plymouth from Parsonage Fields, 1880. A pleasant place to take a stroll, with quite a pastoral scene on this side of the water.

127. A more distant view of the Port Admiral's House, from Mount Wise. It is of particular interest because it is dated January 1876.

128. The Royal Albert Bridge, Brunel's spectacular creation, circa 1880. We see the amount of shipping going up and down the Tamar. On one side of the river is Devon and the other side is Cornwall, the scenery on both banks is very beautiful, a steamer trip up the river has been for many years one of the most delightful outings from Plymouth.

129. The entrance to H.M. Dockyard, Fore Street, Devonport, circa 1885. There were many early Georgian houses here which had grown around the dockyards and the garrison barracks.

130. This huge building was the Royal Albert Hospital, it later became known as the Prince of Wales and then Devonport Hospital. The Victorian costumes are of particular interest. The block has since been demolished and is now a residential area.

131. Another view of the Raglan Barracks, Devonport in the late nineteenth century. They were notable for their tower and portico. Here we see troops on parade.

132. An unusual vista of Mount Edgecumbe House, as it must have looked around 1880. There was much statuary in the formal garden in front of the house, and swans in the surrounding moat. Although much changed today it is still a beautiful and peaceful place, open to the public.

133. A scene from the Hamoaze and Keyham Dock in Victorian days. This is the estuary of the Tamar extending for four miles, a fine harbour up to a mile wide in places, a protected anchorage for vessels of the largest size, as well-known to Drake, Raleigh, Hawkins and their fellow seamen as it is familiar to sailors of today.

134. An idyllic scene taken from the Ruins, Mount Edgecumbe. It shows Drake's Island with the flag flying, and the formidable fortress of the Citadel in the distance. Here we can clearly see the strategic importance of Drake's Island, lying as it does only half a mile from the Hoe, it commands the only two deep-water passages through the Sound.

135. Keyham Dockyard pictured in the days of Queen Victoria. Here ships of every class have been serviced and provisioned through the years by a huge force of dedicated men and women. Devonport Dockyard is probably the biggest ship repair yard in Western Europe, it covers well over 300 acres.

136. For those in search of the picturesque what could have been more romantic than the Barn Pool and the delightful Temple, Mount Edgecumbe. It is not surprising that the genius of J.W. Turner found much inspiration for his painting whilst staying at Mount Edgecumbe House.

137. Here we see the wooded slopes of Mount Edgecumbe from Mount Wise, circa 1880.
The grassy banks of the Mount were obviously a popular place to visit to watch the many
and varied vessels in the Sound. Note the man with the telescope in the foreground.

138. This romantic cameo shows Milton's Temple on the Mount Edgecumbe estate, circa 1880. Framed by the lush foliage and woodland growing right down to the shoreline of the Sound. What a wonderful scene of peace and tranquility.

139. Parsonage Fields, Devonport from another angle, circa 1880. Very few buildings, it
is a country scene in the midst of great activity in the three towns, which were all
expanding at this time.

140. A suitable end to this collection is this photograph of Sir Francis Chichester on board his yacht, Gypsy Moth IV, as he was about to leave Plymouth for London, after his single-handed voyage round the world. He was sailing to London to be knighted by H.M. Queen Elizabeth II. It was at Greenwich that the Queen conferred upon him the honour of knighthood, using the sword of Sir Francis Drake, the sword used by Queen Elizabeth I when she knighted the famous Captain Francis Drake aboard his ship the Golden Hind. Drake was the first Englishman to circumnavigate the globe, Chichester was the first to do so single-handed. The second Sir Francis of whom Plymouth is justly proud.